True Thoughts

ENCOURAGING WORDS
NEW VERSION

B-LIEVE

Copyright © 2024 by B-lieve.

ISBN: 9798890903006 (sc)

All rights reserved. No part of this book may be reproduced or transmitted in any form or by any means, electronic or mechanical, including photocopying, recording, or by any information storage and retrieval system, without permission in writing from the copyright owner.

The views expressed in this work are solely those of the author and do not necessarily reflect the views of the publisher, and the publisher hereby disclaims any responsibility for them.

EXPRESSO Executive Center 777, Dunsmuir Street Vancouver, BC V71K4
1-888-721-0662 ext 101
info@expressopublishing.com

CONTENTS

1. In God We Trust. 1
2. Happy Then Sad. 4
3. Reminder 8
4. Cry 9
5. Every Now And Then. 10
6. Back 11
7. Coming Out The Closet. 12
8. Time. 13
9. Boy Or Man 14
10. Have Notes 15
11. The Reason. 17
12. Tired. 18
13. Close I Get 19
14. Your World. 20
15. Hate \ Love. 22
16. Apologize 23
17. The End 24
18. Their Story 29

June 27, 1971

Icey Jones gave birth to me; I was brought into a world that had a lot of hatred, jealousy, envy and greed - born into a race of people that were not believed to be equal to another race. I came into this world with a pure and innocent heart - trusting, loving and kind, all the attributes of God as I understand Him.

The older I get, the more I learned about this world, this system and how things were run, the colder I become, I started losing my innocent and pure heart. It wasn't based simply on my life but on my people as a whole.

I came from a middle class family. My mother worked hard and long hours to be able to support me and my siblings - a brother and a sister. We always had a place to stay, food and nice things. My biological father wasn't a part of my life.

When I became a teenager, my mother got married; I had another brother and a stepfather. Around that time, I was already set to my own ways. Soon after, I started using alcohol and drugs like most teenagers - just experimenting. Later in life I found out it's called self-medicating, trying to numb my feelings because I didn't know my purpose. I was spiritually starving, confused and my people were getting worse.

As people, we were frightened, demoralized and hopeless. The best thing I could do is getting a job; buy nice things then soon die. Keep living like this forever and act like nothing is wrong, just worry about myself but I figured out that's how the people running things wanted me to think. Division makes it easier for them to keep us under control, I don't blame my people, and it was put in our ancestors to make us think how we think now, just to keep us held down and to make money.

People charges other people money, for something that God provided and let grow naturally. All the resources that are being used will still grow without money, so it's really all about greed - when the people who are selling it killed, lied and betrayed others just to have the power to do it. Now these people try to act so righteous and that makes me mad, I know it makes many of my people mad, too.

The only thing most of us don't know is how to deal with our anger and we're taking it out on each other, but the people with power are acting like money and material things are more valuable than our lives, the lives of the people we love and even if we disagree, there is nothing we can do about it, so most of the time we start believing it ourselves and kill each other over things made by man's hands.

There was a time in my life I wanted to commit suicide and thought what I have to live for - I didn't have a job, a house, a car, nothing but God. I had to sit back, think clearly and asked myself, Isn't God enough? That's when I realized how messed up this world is and how it got into my mind. If it wasn't for my relationship with God, I probably would have killed myself or somebody else just to get some fake material things that has no real value, things that I can't take with me when I die.

Then I thought about those greedy, evil people destroying my people, those who don't care for as long as they can make money and keep control over us. We are more valuable than money and material things, but were made to believe we weren't. I don't know if the damage can be reversed. There are so many people who have killed their selves or somebody, for material things. Too much innocent blood has been shed, God sees it all and He's going to end it. If you don't change the way you think, you're going to go down with them. I didn't write this to say everything's going to be alright nor it's going to be easy, I'm saying it's going to be hard and you're going to have to make some very hard decisions. You're going to have to trust God and be able to go without for a while if need be. We have to understand we're not suffering because of God, we're suffering because of our sins - the decisions we have made. God has given us authority over this land, beast, and evil spirits. The only problem is most of us doesn't know who we really are and pay no attention to God's laws and commands. I don't blame my people because our identity has been stolen and we've been brought to this foreign land. Most of our ancestors even up to this day, our leaders, preachers, and prophets have not separated themselves from the people of this land as regards their detestable things and their way of life.

A holy seed has become mingled and tangled up with an unholy seed. We've come to believe and think as they do, and our leaders lead us to follow in this unfaithfulness. It's gotten to the point that we have more fear in man's laws than God's laws, but the good thing is God has not left us even if we turned our backs to His laws and commandments. All we have to do is turn back to God and learn how to follow His laws and commandments.

Stop working for their peace and their prosperity - in order for us people have a strong relationship with God and be able to see things spiritually, then truly live spiritually.

I, myself don't believe in religion but I'm not mad at anyone who does believe. I believed that God made a new covenant with His children, that He was going to put His spirit in us and if you're one of His children you have that spirit in you.

You don't need any man to tell you. I'm not trying to judge anyone because I never think I'm better than anyone, I know I'm not perfect but I believe I should be given the same right to be able to feel, think and live for what I believe in. I'm not mad nor I hate nor do I want to kill anybody.

I used to think I was mad but I found out it was really about feeling hurt. As a man I didn't want to admit I was hurt and confused because I was scared that would make me look weak. I hid it off by acting like everything is alright even though it's really not. I would rather go somewhere, drink and get high instead of telling somebody I'm hurt, confused and needed help.

Finally, I admitted I needed help so I went to a drug treatment center. There, a lot of people have the same feelings but don't know what to do. It was good for me; I got to understand my feelings better and was able to talk about it openly among brothers who could relate to it and be able to share some with me. It was encouragement and support. I, once again had hope - you could be yourself and that gave me a chance to get to know myself better. I realized I've only got power over myself. We used to say the serenity prayer in the morning and at night, [God grant me the serenity to accept the things I cannot change the courage to change the things I can and the wisdom to know the difference] and He gave me the wisdom.

If only I have power over myself, I will change the ways I think and react right now, everything else I don't worry about.

Like the past, everybody knows about how we have been treated. From being kidnapped into slavery and everything else up to this day. I've seen documents, movies, heard songs and stories about many unimaginable things like it's alright and how publicly acknowledged it was. I remembered I used to sit around drinking and getting high, listening to people complaining about how bad our situation was, sitting around talking like it's over, like the story never ends but when are we going to be able to say it until this happened and that ended it.

Most of the time when I hear one of my people talking about it and complaining on how we can do it kind of way, but I never heard a solution. I'm not saying I got the solution but I don't think we will be able to beat them at their own game. I think that the bus boycott in 1965 when we stop riding the buses for over a year was more effective than any of the riots and I think the solution is going to come in that type of form. When I hear the people with power talk about what we've been through, I think they have a lot of nerve. Like they openly say what they have done and what are you going to do about it. They don't even try to hide it, like we've done it and what are you going to do about it. You better be happy, you can do what you can today and I think that's wrong. I'm not mad because we are the ones who accepted it and kept going along with it.

Remember we only have power over our own actions. I believe that they want to make us mad, for us to doubt ourselves because that messes with the way we act and carry ourselves. That's why we can't do it out of anger; we have to do it because it's right to want the same for our people as they want for theirs. Don't get me wrong, I'm not talking about no skin color, or if it's a spiritual thing and if you have that spirit in you - you're going to know who I'm talking about. But that's what it's about - a righteous and justice system. It's not about no revenge or no hate;it's about what's right and trying to stop a cycle that's getting worse and worse every generation. You can throw the past out the window and you could still see that my people aren't getting treated right today. Then there's so many arguments about if there's a God or not and if the Bible is real or not, and I do believe that there's a God, but even if there wasn't if everybody followed the ten commandments, the world would be a better place - so I don't see what's all the arguments about. I guess so they can chase the wants of their own heart - lie, steal, kill, have sex with anybody and not feel guilty. We are living among some evil and wicked people. Every generation is getting wicked than the last, getting farther and farther away from God's laws, for the people who don't believe in God's righteousness.

Morals have been replaced with greed; they got us focused on things we can see rather than the unseen. When the things seen perish and the unseen are everlasting. When the body dies, it turns back into dust but the spirit is for eternity. Material things can be stolen, lost, or rust away but what you did to get them will have an effect on your spirit forever. What good is it to gain the world but to lose your soul? I was taught that when you get married and have sexual relations, your partner receives a piece of your spirit and you receive a part of theirs, making you and them become one and I believe that. But there are so many people having sex with different people that they aren't married to - just for fun. Not realizing that each person you have sex with is taking apart of your spirit and you are taking a part of theirs. So a lot of people have so many different spirits up in them. They start to go crazy, have mood swings and lose perspective of their true identity. Everything God put here for us, we demoralize it. A lot of people took advantage of it, turned it into something that wasn't meant to be. They complicate something that is so simple a child can understand. God loves His children, so why would He make you figure out a riddle to know Him?

When I was in rehab, the counselor showed us a picture; he went around the room and asked everybody what they saw. Everybody saw something different (whatever that they took from it) but we were all wrong. The answer was a picture. People try to read so much into something and be so intelligent that they make something so simple become so hard. That's why my poems are simple and I write simply because I don't want people to try to read more into them than what it is or be amazed at the various words I use. I want a child or even one with very little education to be able to understand what I mean. Most people, professors, scholars and the smart type aren't going to have an open mind. They want scientific facts or hard evidence like I was before. They focus more on the scene. However, it was written that this faithless generation will be giving no more signs. Their forefathers were giving signs and miracles and they still didn't believe. Like I said, it's a spirit inside you that's going to know the truth and you're going to know without a sign. You just have to trust God and know that His spirit is inside of you - so you have to trust that spirit inside of you. Learn who you really are and realize that you are just part of a body. You might be a foot, a toe, an arm, a hand, a finger, a muscle, a bone, or a vein, but whatever you are, you're just as important as the rest of the body and they are just as important as you. Humble yourself and concentrate on the function you are supposed to perform. Let everybody do their own function and concentrate on doing yours. If you're the foot, don't try to be the hand, and don't try to tell the hand how it's supposed to function because they are meant to function different from you. You have to trust it and concentrate on fulfilling your part. Support the rest of the body, encourage it. Don't judge it and don't try to make them do things just because that's the way you function but because it wasn't meant to be like that. That doesn't mean you're more important or they are. You both have your own function that has its own responsibility to make His body work how it was supposed to coordinate, let the left foot take the first step and let right follow, march forward and let the blood flow through the veins into the heart, giving life bringing forth the brain the ability to open up, to be able to think on God's way, so we can concentrate on exercising our muscles to build up the strength to let the hands grab it and finally take control, as a whole. One accords all parts in unity. Think about it - no more jealousy, envy, hatred, confusion, division in the body. We will all be doing what God wants us to do for the purpose of making the body function together, and not the wants of our own hearts. We can't be selfish, we have to be considerate of the rest of the body and do what's best for it as a whole. Understand laws were made for us; we were not made for laws. I feel now they're getting used to controlling my people. They are certainly not for the honor of God because they were made by men whose values are not the same as our God. They feel their forefather's laws are more important than the lives of God's children, and they're being judged with an unbalanced scale by people that are not perfect themselves. They put a burden on the poor people that they themselves couldn't bear if they were in their situation. It's funny how their job is to make laws and decisions for people who do not think like them and do not have the same wants. Their lifestyle is so different from ours, they have not faced the challenges we face, but they still judge and make decisions for us. I can't understand it but it's not my job to. I just trust my Father and speak the words I'm supposed to. It's not just His children they've done badly; they're mistreating mother earth as well.

I believe we were put here to take care of the earth but they misuse its resources for their own gain. God sees it and He's mad. We were made for the Earth; the Earth wasn't made for us. We're all going to die but the earth is still going to be here. So we should treat it with respect and stop taking it for granted. We act like our luxuries are more important than the earth itself.

There's been a lot of talk about global warming yet people pay no attention. They want to have fancy cars, big houses, have fun but they don't realize without the earth none of that could exist and without God's spirit inside of us, we wouldn't exist - so then their laws wouldn't exist. However, they act like their laws and their money is more important, but they would be meaningless without us.

I wrote a poem about waking up and being the only person on earth and in it I asked the questions "how would I know good from bad and what would I like if nobody told me this is what's popular or that is bad?". I believe God will still be in me, and the earth will still supply me with my needs. Then I realized it's the people that make it hard. They have you do so much to get something that's already right there. They have us trying to please them when they can't be pleased. You will never be able to do enough, because they're just humans and it's in their hearts to never be satisfied. So they're going to keep putting more and more pressure on us until it breaks, and my people's eyes will be opened to see that you are ruling them with fake power.

They're taking credit for something they are not capable of making happen. They cannot stop this world from producing its resources and they definitely cannot send you to heaven or hell. They aren't doing nothing but playing middle man, that is taking something that's free and put a price on it, then charge other humans when they're just humans also, that has no more rights to it than us. The bad thing is it's enough for everybody, but greed and men traditions over God's children. "Do you think God would be happy for us to proclaim a religion, dress in the finest clothes, sit in the best seats and say the loudest prayer? Or if we have nothing but still treated His children right?-And realize that what He want is for us to live for Him and how you live for Him is to love His children and walk with them, not ahead of them". That's what it's all about. It's going to a lot of people hollering Lord, but He's going to answer - He doesn't know you.

It's not about religion; it's a way of life. You can't live for this world and live for Him, you're going to love one more. I'm not trying to judge nobody, I'm just saying "wouldn't it make more sense to let everybody live without money because everything will still grow?" - We can still pump oil and gas, electricity will still flow, and everything would still work. Who do they pay for these things to happen, not God, the earth, the sun, or the moon? Whose face is on their money, so give them theirs, but give God His, let mean His children.

[When did I mistreat You, when you did it to anyone of My children you also do it to God], is a saying I was taught. Love your neighbor as you love yourself.

It seems so simple that you know it is someone who's making it this hard. Just because that's all we know that we don't make it, that's the way it supposed to be.

I mean you have to have an open mind to see past the boundaries placed in our minds by traditions and rituals. A way of life that really might not be the way it was supposed to be but we accepted it because that's all we know, that's all we were taught and that's how we get rewarded or punished. So that's what we go by with no questions asked, without considering the purpose, the reason, the effects, or cost. I'm not talking about their money; I'm talking about your spirit, your relationship with God and the people that get hurt and the damage to the earth and atmosphere. Who knows the outcome? - I don't but I don't believe they don't neither, so I'd rather trust me and go by what I see, than what they tell me, because people do lie and deceive to get what they want and that's what I see. A system set up to strive off of other people's misfortunes and wrong doings, so it's not even in their best interest to see it stop. So I can't wait or expect them to change, that wouldn't be in their or my best interest.

I have three beautiful daughters (Brittany, Shaniqua, and Destiney) and a loving wife (Chantea), and I thank God for them. They are special, they are my gifts, and they gave me a new perspective in life. I looked at women differently and how one day they're going to have children and their children are going to have children and so on.

When I die that's not going to be the end of things, God opened my eyes to be able to see the bigger picture and understand it's not just about me. I'm just a piece of a puzzle, so I have to look past me and focus on the whole puzzle, just find my place and take it. I can't let my body stop me because my God is a God of the living and the body is going to die but He will still be the God of my spirit. I believe He will so He is the God of my spirit not my body. My body is a tool being used to persuade my spirit that it is more important than it, when eventually it dies but the spirit can't be killed, it's for eternity. The body turns back into dust, if you're lucky in about 70 or 80 years, or a lot lesser or a few more, but you do understand eternity - it's never ending, it doesn't even have a number. That's what I'm talking about, something happening that's not been done yet. It's not a word made for it, it can't be compared to anything I've ever seen so I can't explain it because it's beyond our vocabulary. How the blind see, the deaf hear, the lamb walk, it's when your spirit is set free. When we really learn to live spiritually and I believe it's going to happen here on earth.

TRUE THOUGHTS

We will no longer have to wait until after we die, I can't tell you exactly how or when but I'm learning to trust My Father God and do my part without knowing or expecting an outcome, just speaking about the desperate need for a start of the process to make the change. I'm just acting like a horn blowing, hoping God's children hear it and answer the calling, not literally but you know what I mean. I am in no way saying I'm better than anyone else or know more than everybody else. I do believe I have a good relationship with our Father God and that's what this speaking about. I learned about Him and what He put in my heart, I know I'm not the only one. There are a lot of us out there and the time has come for us to come together with an open mind to see past these barricades placed around our minds and past some of these disagreements that are keeping us separated. A lot of us share the same goal; we just have different methods of getting there. Our pride and us trying to prove that we know more and that your religion or race is supreme over all others, when we really are all children of God by faith and there is no faith in laws, can't understand that.

Power is in unity, if you have a million people and each had a dollar you all will have a million dollars and out of that million each one is going to know a trade. You're going to have doctors, lawyers, teachers, farmers and so on. With each one using their trade to support the body and not for false riches, see that everything will still happen but the poor, the fatherless child, and widows will be taken care of. The only thing stopping them from having something is due to people charging us for something that's already ours. I feel it would be easier for everybody to drop to the bottom instead of everybody to try climb to the top. Because everybody is not going to be able to climb to the top and the ones that can leave the ones that need them. They start to look down on them instead of eye to eye. They forget and some never knew how it feels to be at the bottom. We're a body and the weaker parts need the strength and support of the stronger parts because that's how it was meant to be. Some were meant to be soldiers, some farmers, some teachers, healers and so on.

Everybody have their own purpose but it's for the strength of the body. It's not what you do it's for what reason. I'm not asking you to change your life. I'm asking you to do what you do for this purpose and not the purpose of chasing after their false riches. Just consider the possibility that we don't need to ignore the ones who needs us, just to pay people that have no control over the seasons changing, the sun shining, the rain falling, crops growing, or natural resources flowing. They are charging us for something that do not belong to them, and the bad thing is it had us killing one another, hating, envying, committing adultery, fornicating, stealing, but most of all, putting it before God. It had you breaking all God's laws and separated us, so the body can't function the way it was meant to. For something that's fake, that was made up by some evil, greedy, wicked people for the purpose of them to keep their power and control - that's the only purpose and goal. So you have to see it from that point of view.

Understand the reason behind the things we are taught and are made to believe for the purpose of the people teaching you the way it is supposed to be, when you know you were never taught anything but how to fit into a system that was created and meant to keep their power and control, continues without us figuring out that the power is fake. That you are putting unnecessary stress on God's children to make them fit into something they were not meant to fit in. For things that brings us no true satisfaction because they don't know the truth, instead of keep trying to do something, to achieve something that really don't exist, but has the power to make it more valuable than God's own children and that's the biggest problem. That's what this book is really about- rebuilding God's temple, blowing a horn for God's children to come back together as one. For one purpose to make the body strong - the beginning of a righteous but ruthless era.

I believe the time has come for it to begin. Take that first step to identify the members of the body. Everything that happened to you in your life already gave you the knowledge and experience you need. Now it's time to come together and use it to support the body. It sound so easy, you don't have to do any rituals, celebrate a certain day, and you don't have to pay no money because we can't buy our way out of what we're in. All we have to do is put our pride, jealousy, and self-righteousness to the side, and unite as one, one body on the same accord. It's so simple yet so hard to love your brothers and sisters and appreciate their value. I found out that anything is possible when we work together; even changing the situation we're in. I believe we can and will change this system. The body is gone, come together and God is gone, and do the rest.

I don't know exactly how or what's going to happen. I believe my job is to blow the horn and call God's children together. I'm not trying to teach, just reach and give you a feeling in your spirit that opens your mind up to see past what you were taught. Realize and believe that there is a better way to live as people. We don't have to do the things we're doing to each other and ourselves for something that's fake. We are the money; let them have their money because we don't need it. We can do everything they charge us, for without it, all we need is each other and that's the key.

Once we come together we can actually burn the money, we wouldn't need it anymore. We don't need to waste our time trying to figure how to make it; we need to concentrate on uniting the body, that's the most important thing because that's going to be the power. Take the value out of their money because their power strives on us believing that fake piece of paper is our God. That it is what makes this world go, when it really is God. We have to understand, believe, trust and live by that. Full heartedly and no more meaningless talk. It's time to take your position, it's going to happen but why not come together over a million people hollering can't be ignored. The sound will make the walls fall then we can demand our needs and not buy them. They can't arrest, kill, and punish everybody. That's why we need all His Children!

IN GOD WE TRUST

I'm getting hard and stubborn as I'm watching this world turn into one of sin, where men pretend to be a friend until that thick turns thin, that's when reality kicks in, "O" Lord' where shall we begin, what about when You first made men when we got lonely You then made women, they made mistakes but You still let the first family begin, when, You could of just stopped it then, so it got to be a purpose and a way to win, but it seems like everybody just gave in to the life of sin, the juice and gin, every man for man, it's hard to get a helping hand, especially when they don't understand that they're falling into the devil's plan do you even know God's ten commands, not one or two but all ten?

If you don't, you're letting the devil win, so you better begin before the end because I know what God intends to do with the devil and his friends and if you think it's worth it, think again, you have to let go of the selfishness, the jealousy, the pride, the hate, the envy, and all your world desires, and replace them with love, faith, trust, hope, encouragement and overall peace, with this kind of unity, with everyone's mind on the same page we can all try to make it through this maze cuz we're starting to run out of days, I know it's hard to change your ways but you'll be amazed if you just praised the 'Lord' even though things aren't going your way, you'll find out things are still okay, just pray, don't go stray, remember God's words and try your best to obey, if you slip don't trip you got to keep trying until that final day, the devils gonna try to tempt you a lot of different ways every single day, he don't play on your weaknesses he prey, he'll make you think your way is the right way, make you not care what God has to say especially when it contradicts with your life style that's when you say you're gonna wait awhile until you're ready to change, that's when God's "number you'll dial and that's so foul, what if your child got buck wild?

Would you want them to hide, try to deceive, and to lie or would you want them to come to you and tell you why? so you can help them try to get by and you'll never give up on them till the day they die, and that's the same way with 'Father God', the fact that we're 'His' children is something we disregard and it's really so simple but we make it so hard, it's time for us to take charge and to find the light, gotta quit betting this world tell us what's wrong or right, who gave them the insight to say what's foul or tight and to be perfect you gotta be a certain weight and height?

Do they have power do they have 'God's' might?

Can they control the moon and stars and make them shine every night? A man is just a man, rich, poor, fat or thin, so it's impossible to think you are able to do what 'God' can, so then what makes you better than all the other men when God made you the same way He made them, if your way is the right way, show me proof and if you can't find it in the Bible then it's not the truth.

TRUE THOUGHTS

It's just your opinion, something that makes you happy, I don't care if you learned it from your mama or your daddy, God is the only One that can tell you how it suppose to be.

How can you when you don't even know me?

Did you pay a fee to set me free?

Did you give your blood so that we could have a relationship with Father God the Almighty?

So don't try to take credit like you did this good deed. Like a rose that looks so beautiful, they even know they wouldn't be if someone didn't plant their seed, and how smarter are we if we could just get over all this jealousy, and envy, and all of us agree that if it wasn't for God' none of us would be. So whose body is this when I didn't make or buy me? It's God's body He just let my mind be free to decide if I want to live or die, laugh or cry, tell the truth or lie, give in or try to win this race, set myself at a steady pace to come in Heaven even if I don't come in first place.

HAPPY THEN SAD

To make one happy you make another sad, some steal, even kill if they wanted what you had.

Why? Don't you know the difference between good and bad?

What makes God smile? What makes 'God' mad?

We gotta be patient through this short life of ours and realize it's not about sex, having parties and driving them fancy cars.

It's deeper than that, it's a well known fact, that one day soon Jesus is coming back and He's not gonna care about how much money you got.

You cannot lie or buy your way into God's Kingdom the only way to get there is thorough 'Jesus Christ God's beloved Son, so don't be dumb and think you can get in by the good deeds you have done.

If so, was it for fun? Why did Jesus even have to come down to Earth?

What was the meaning of His birth?

TRUE THOUGHTS

A sinless man, yeah that's the first, they couldn't understand it so at Him they spit and curse.

The pain He felt had to be the worst. But He took it, the ultimate sacrifice, could you have paid that price, to get treated bad and still act nice?

Having the strength to be able to live a sinless life; you think it's easy when you know you're about to die and still have faith in God so you refuse to tell a lie?

Whoa; You are so precious My savior Jesus Christ, went through all that pain, and what did You have to gain?

Didn't care about the fame, but had to fulfill the law and honor God's name.

'You' knew your purpose, You knew what needed to be done, put all sins on your back and sacrificed for everyone.

You are truly God's son, You died and still yet You won, three days later, again You walked under the sun, defeated death, gave hope through the resurrection, but do people even remember what You have done?

Do they take it serious or do they want to just have fun?

Santa clause and the Easter bunny gets more credit than God's own Son.

And when were they born and where are they from?

B-LIEVE

Do they believe in God in the land of make believe?

Do they eat? Do they sleep? Does God take care of their needs?

Any and everything, you can hear, smell, feel, or see was created by Father God the Almighty, and if it wasn't for Him none of this could be.

So give credit where credit is due.

He made you, everybody knows this is true.

He loves you so much only if you knew.

When you get weak lean on Him and He will carry you through.

But everybody says the time has not come, while their fixing up their fancy houses instead of rebuilding God's Holy One.

Think about what you have done.

How can one have all the riches and another have none?

Look how selfish and greedy a lot of people have become.

You have love for the rich but despise the poor and dumb, and if money is printed by a machine, make more, give everybody some, that's all become one and rebuild the temple of God the All Powerful One.

Be Brave; Be Brave; is what God say;

TRUE THOUGHTS

He gave us Ten Commands that we have to learn to obey. And it can be done, we just have to take it day by day and before long it will be peace and the place we stay, so I pray.

REMINDER

I'm not here to be a teacher, I'm just simply here to remind you of when you were innocent and your heart was still pure but you had to mature, you learned about war, you got a little money so that made you want more, just looking for that big score, so fathers became pimps and mothers became whores everybody wants to be rich they say there's no respect for the poor, it's all about sex and money ain't that's what you're living for? But think about when you were just four, you were happy with getting some bubble gum from the candy store, when you didn't have to work, didn't even have to do no chores just played with your toys feeling safe behind them closed doors, in your own little world life was so easy, dreaming about what you want to be, even if you were a slave, you thought you were free.

CRY

Cry, cry everyday, waking up thinking about problems from yesterday so that increases your chances of making more problems today and if things keep going that way, you're gonna solve a problem but create a problem day after day, it's like a game so all you do is play but you were never taught the rules you were suppose to obey coz you don't go by what God say, we've all been led astray, our heritage and beliefs have been taken away, in public schools you're not even allowed to pray.

They teach us about the people that freed us from being slaves but what about before we became slaves? Why can't you teach us about them ways?

Did we believe in God is that who we praised?

But now it seems like we're in a craze, coz even though it don't feel right we still try to do it just because we were taught that way.

EVERY NOW AND THEN

Every now and then I like grin, play have fun but it's hard when the world is full of sin little girl only ten get kidnapped and raped by wicked, evil men while mothers in the club drinking juice and gin, daddy's drunk off that hen, he snapped now he's in the state pen so the system steps in like they're your next of kin and pretend to be your friend teach you your ABC's and how to count to ten but you still don't fit in just don't feel like no American citizen so there's an empty space deep within was never taught love all they teach is how to sin cut on the news and somebody just got killed again, and again, and again, turn the channel you might see Barbie having sex with Ken then want us to pick Democrat or Republican, but who represents the African man? Who can?

Not them, especially when we're the descendants of Abraham and God gave us this land, why can't you understand, you cannot change God's plan, this is not a game your playing, please listen to what I'm saying everyone turn to the same page so we can all sing the same hymn, everyone on the same cord, Oh; how powerful it would sound then, Father God would be so happy, I just wish I could see Him grin, and I know it's time to begin to honor His name the best I can.

BACK

Don't look back coz it's a trap it's a known fact when you do that you can't go forward coz it like distract your mind and it throws your life off track and that's when the devil attack and he'll use anything, he'll use crack, alcohol, sex, movies like the Mack have everybody driving a Cadillac but I laugh at that but it's not funny coz it got blacks killing blacks, everyday for that money, happy if you get a stack, not even caring that Jesus is coming back then what?

What you gone do grab your strap?

Huh! You gone give Him a sack?

Do you think your money will have an impact?

or do you think He's gonna ask? Why didn't you look forward to me instead of looking back? Forever!!!!!!!!

COMING OUT THE CLOSET

Coming out the closet coz there's nothing to be ashamed of, I make a lot of mistakes, but I see a lot of mistakes and yet still show you love, so what should I be scared of, you saying something bad about me, you looking at me mean, it might hurt my feelings, but do feelings really mean anything?

I'm a soldier in God's army, you can in no way harm me, even if you kill me, you still cannot take my spirit see it belongs to God!

And as long as I do my job, to tell everyone that God is mad coz their hearts are so hard, the wicked and evil are gonna get their due. You're gonna be punished, man only if you knew, God don't want to do it that's why Jesus was sent to save you, it's not too late, you can ask God in Jesus name to forgive you and He will coz His mercy is so great!

But your heart has to be sincere, your prayer can't be fake, that don't mean you're not gonna have bad days but God is going to help you overcome your mistakes, so come on soldiers stand up for God's sake!!

TIME

You have to acknowledge time and don't take for granted its value then you will be able to find that what you spend it on today is gonna effect what happens down the line so right now, this minute, we have to start using our mind please listen because this is serious I'm not just trying to rhyme, I got three daughters 15, 13, and 9 and if you love yours like I love mine, for the kids sake that's all combine our efforts and our knowledge we learned thorough time and let God use us as a light to shine on the path that don't led them to drugs and crime because my first time going to jail was in 1989 and the judge said "he give me 2 years" but he actually took 2 years of my time and once you lose that time it's gone forever it's something you will never find so you have to realize that nothing is free you pay for crime with time!

BOY OR MAN

When does a boy become a man is what I'm trying to understand, is it when you believe in yourself and stick to your game plan to the end because no matter how it looks you know you're still gonna win, when you don't think about what nobody else thinks coz you're surviving by the works of your own hands, when everybody thinks it's right but you don't think it's right and you take a stand, not even caring about what somebody else is saying, coz you know you're a man of God even though everybody else thinks you're just playing but not hearing at night when you be praying!

HAVE NOTES

What about the have nots the ones living and dying just trying to get what you got and even though you have a lot they still have to resort to selling some rocks and some dope spot worrying about trying to stack a knot so much that somehow you forgot they invest a lot of our money into them cops and we pay them very well for them three meals and them cots, so who will it really hurt if this cycle stops

I'm telling you they depend just as much as you do on them dope drops they depend on them gun shots coz without that they couldn't get paid for patrolling our blocks and their prisons would become empty lots

it's just not enough money in them routine traffic stops and that's the reason they set up and they plot and scheme and try to entrap the have nots and it works because we're so distracted by trying to figure out how to get what they got that we forgot 'God' is what we got and they can't make that in no factory or they machine shop, and that's something they ain't got

yeah money and material things they might have a lot but God is something that can't be made or bought so without God they really are the have nots.

And they're trying to trick me out of what I know I got But no I'm not selling or trading my assigned spot

In heaven where a lot is going to be a little and a little is gonna be a lot.

THE REASON

What's the reason? What's the purpose? Why are we even breathing?

Why are we believing everything that we're seeing when people can be so deceiving and they mislead and they pretend that they love but they have hate deep within, we were all born into sin, when Eve bit that fruit it happened then, so who can show us how to win?

Not even the smartest men would be able to do it only God can, no matter if you're the president or a preacher, your still just a man who's no better then any other man but you just don't understand because sometimes power distracts your mind and you forget the plan, but God put this situation in your hand it's nothing but a test you've just been blessed but it's not just for you it's for you to bring up the rest and the man with the most money isn't always the best.

TIRED

I'm so tired but I can't stop coz I'm almost there, even though it seems so far away like I'm not really going no where, just going through trials and tribulations thinking life's not fair, but God said, How dare you let this world scare My children when you know that I care and I won't give you a burden that you are unable to bear, I'll lift it off you if you ask in a sincere prayer, but along the line somewhere you forgot that I am everywhere and the same respect and love you have in a church, you should have here, because I am also there!

CLOSE I GET

The closer I get to the Almighty Lord the more the devil try his hardest to discourage me but he can't see, because I know what God wants me to be and I know that it's not going to be easy I know the devil is going to try to tempt me, I know he's gonna try to deceive me coz he wants me to believe that I'm a hypocrite, a loser, I'm just an alcoholic and a drug user, he wants to take away my hope everyday he wants me to drink and smoke and treat life like a big joke and I was letting him do it like a dope, the more I sinned the more I ran, making excuses, hiding when God was there holding out His hand but all I knew was the life of sin and tell you the truth I liked it back then, but when God let me be His friend and showed me how the world began and how He made all men, in the Bible it says He wants all to win all you have to do is turn to Him and repent for your sin but that's when the devil steps in to try to stop you anyway he can, that's when you're gonna have to get wisdom so you can learn to understand, you have to control your sinful desires, we have to stick to the game plan and realize that we are a precious gem, no matter how you look or how much money you got as long as you believe in Him then you will understand respect for the Lord and you will find that you know God, He protects the innocent but that don't mean life's not gonna be hard, you're still going to have problems but God's gonna give you the wisdom to understand!

YOUR WORLD

What if you lived on earth by yourself, who would care about your jewels or your wealth? who would you shine for? Who could you impress?

Think for a minute, then tell me if you think you can pass this test, You wake up and there's nobody in sight, Do you think you would have the might to survive by yourself, do you know how to make light?

How would you know the difference between day and night?

Who could you get mad, who could you fight?

Who would care if you done wrong or right?

Do you think you would do the same things you do today?

How could you make it if there's nobody to show you the way?

Who could you talk to, what can you say?

I bet you can still talk to God if you pray. Who could you own, who can give you advice?

TRUE THOUGHTS

Would you even know the difference between mean and nice?

Can you have something that don't have a price?

Can you plant your own red beans an

Do you think you can make a car from scrap?

If you did, do you think you would make rims or hub caps?

If you take a trip, would you first make a map?

What would you live for, there's no one to impress anymore,

Whoa, think about it, what would you live for?

Then live for it.

HATE \ LOVE

I hate myself sometimes but yet still I love God so much that even when I don't understand I still must trust and no matter what I must never give up, I must stop saying if, but, making excuses setting myself up for bad luck because yet still it is God who I trust so I must be able to tell the difference between love and lust and must learn to communicate without having to cuss, I must not just sit back, complain, and fuss until the very day I turn back into dust, but yet still even then it's God who I will trust!

APOLOGIZE

I apologize for the last time, because I have suicidal thoughts crossing my mind.

But I know God, so I know I'll be committing a true crime if I give up when God said look for Me in there the answer you'll find. And why should 'T feel pity when you cry and whine,

When all you have to do is come back to Me and sincerely try to get your life back on line?

And quit living for the wants of your own heart and live for the rights of Mine.

I sent messengers, even my own beloved Son. I shouldn't have to give you another sign.

Look at the moon and how the sun, off one source, both shine. And all your super stars combined in the height of their prime Can't be able to generate a light as bright as Mine, but yet they're the ones that you let influence your mind.

THE END

In order for something to end it first has to begin.

So, I'm calling for all the righteous men, but Satan says you will not even be able to find ten and that's when I pictured him saying it with a devilish grin so then I grabbed some paper and my pen and I begin to write this poem calling for all righteous men yes we need you all so I had to repeat that again coz I hope these words are being heard by at least ten righteous men that knows ten that also knows ten, that loves God enough to at least try to defend His name not saying that they're gonna be perfect coz we're all going to sin, but they're going to have a spirit of God deep within and on that you're going to learn to depend and then you'll be able to comprehend and look deeper than a trend studying God's laws is what I recommend and then you'll be able to understand why these things are happening and learn the purpose of something the reason it began and then you'll be able to begin to repent from your sin so we can break this cycle we're trapped in and hopefully one day our kids will be able to see the end of what today we begin.

Please, you have to believe. We were put here for a purpose; we were giving a plan by God to achieve. But we all must hear and understand the same plan so every woman and man can put aside their pride and humble ourselves, so we can unite and stand for one purpose, one plan. Not just yours but God's purpose, His plan. Everybody think it can't be done, but with faith and trust it can. If we finally, do it together. Not just for you but for all so we all can win. We need the Holy Spirit to help us to overcome our sin. We don't have to rob, steal, rape, beat, cheat, deceive, lie, and kill one another. We all brothers and sisters, we supposed to do all for each other. We suppose to fight, help, and stand for one another. We do have an enemy but it's not your brother or your sister. But because that's all we see and it's easier to get to each other. That's why we take our anger and madness out on each other. Because we don't even see or know our real enemies. We're taking and even killing each other for something that other somewhere else in a building it's over a million more of the same things. That makes no sense, why kill each other for one thing. Instead of getting together with one another and going to get the million. We need to come together and realize we are valuable. Stop believing what this evil and greedy people we don't even know, tell us what's valuable. They got us thinking money is more valuable than ourselves.

When they burning old money and printing new money, how can they burn something so valuable and then just be able to print more, and say they owe. Mostly everything we kill each for don't even last long and it's being made every day. It's not worth our lives but they have us believing it is. It's crazy because they got us killing each other over something they know it's million more out here. We can't see that one of our soldiers is dead, the other most of the time end up in jail. Two of our soldiers are gone, and it don't happen just once it happens over and over again every day. We helping them, we following their plan. Because that's the only plan we know, but GOD has a plan for us that most of us don't know about or just don't care about. But without our own plan, we will never get of following us enemies' plans. When we die it's still going

It's been along time coming but things gone change. We really don't understand, in our mind, we think we're insane. But over 400 years ago these thoughts were planted in our brain. We were taught to believe we were just slaves and the masters had all the power. That they could do anything to us they wanted to. They could kill, rape, sell, or just separate our families. Who could we run to, we couldn't look, talk back, eat, sit, do nothing with them. A lot of our ancestors died trying to take a stand. But most of our generation don't understand what our ancestors went through, we just saw a couple of movies. We just happy they gave us some privileges our ancestors didn't have. But we still not equal, we still don't have anybody to go to when we're mistreated. Who we have to go to the same people that mistreated us. I see and hear a lot of people marching and saying black lives matter. It sound good and it's a start but what's the goal. Who do they want to start to believe it, the police, the government, the judges, or ourselves. Because it seem like we don't believe it, the way we kill each other. But that's a different story, we mostly go to jail when we do it and they don't. Is that the goal for them to go to jail, or for them to stop killing us?

Do we want our own police and our own government? I just want to know the goal, like I said it's a good start to see so many people come together for something. But it done happen before and it changed a little bit, but we all need the same goal. We need a shepherd to lead the sheep. Like when Moses was sent by 'God' to pharaoh the king of Egypt. God wanted Moses to get His people free, and to go start a new life, a new government, a new way of living, God's way. God has a goal for HIS people and we need a goal. We we're supposed to be freed from slavery, but we still in same place, under same rulership. Our goal was just to be treated equal. Not to control something, own something, or have a say in something. We didn't have high enough goals. Now if they just say they believe black lives matter, send the police to jail, and act like they care. Will that make us happy? They still gone have control over us. We need to say let my people go. I don't care if you think my life matter or not. You shouldn't have the power to be able to be the judge over that. Give us our own land, when we we're supposed to be set free, we were supposed to get 40 acres and a mule. Let us create our own society. Let us live under our own government, our own laws, our own police, our own thoughts, beliefs, our own everything.

That's what we call free. We not free if we still living under your laws, your beliefs, your way of life. We're still under your control. All of us can say something is right or wrong. But it's up to you to make the decision. No matter how many of us say it's wrong, you have the power to say it's right. Don't matter what we think it relies on what you think and we can't do nothing but accept it. We complain and do whatever you say (sound like a slave). I don't know how it's going to change. I have belief and faith in GOD, that HE has to be in the center of it, and we all must believe, trust, and learn HIS plan, then set a goal. A big GOD goal and not believe everything they tell us. We have to somehow reprogram our minds. Erase everything, they taught us because we were taught it to hurt and control us. We say it but I think most of us don't even believe black lives matter (money matters more). I don't think we know how to or what it means. We weren't taught how to live like it, GOD, we need YOU to send the next Moses to lead us to our promised land. Because we keep asking them over and over again and it's not working. It has to be took.

THEIR STORY

They teach us something and they say it's our history, but it really is their story. One that gives them all the glory. One that emphasizes the fact that they always have had authority over people like you and me. Painting a false image to make us believe in their supremacy. But they haven't proven that to me. I know my Father, the GOD of Abraham, Isaac, and Jacob, the true Almighty. The One who was, who is and still to come. While they talking about some 1863 Abraham Lincoln signed a paper that set slaves free. Like it was that easy, because if someone saw you as a slave before he signed that paper, why afterward it wouldn't be a slave they still see. How can a simple man's signature change another man's perception of me. Like I said exaggerating just to prove they had that kind of authority. But in them it's not GOD that I see. They're too greedy, they steal my Father's GOD righteous glory. But they can't no longer see. Because that, that has been stolen from me, my Father GOD has purchased back for me, and all His children. Today 10-19-06, we have to understand what it means to be free, before we really can be. First, we need to come together spiritually and let GOD be the base of our unity. Then maybe eventually, we would be able to communicate.

So, we can come together mentally, so we can stop trying to figure out a mystery and concentrate on what's plan to see, that what hurts us the most is our stupidity. Not talking about 123, ABC, college degree, I'm talking about the loyalty, the fear and love for Father GOD the Almighty. Because there is a possibility, to create the opportunity to make it to the next step coming together physically. Because there is no way possible it's going to change out of sympathy. So, we must collectively come together as a body of one. Spiritually, Mentally, then Physically. Because our GOD is an awesome GOD and if you agree. Let's let their story be their history, but let us learn, teach; fight to write about our story. So, our kids, kids, kids can understand what it means to be free!

Who told you what to believe? Who told you what was good or bad? What was pretty or ugly? What do we base what we believe on from? I think it started from the slave masters. They put it in our ancestors and it came down from generation to generation. Then they start teaching us things in school, on tv and movies. But it all started from when we were slaves. Then the civil war to free slaves, then the civil rights movement and a lot of stories about how good they were, and anybody that tried to help us got killed. I have never heard nothing about how we were before we became slaves. It seems like our lives started when we became slaves, nothing before that. It might be some ways to find out but they didn't tell or teach us that. All we were taught was we were brought over in ships and were slaves. Not how we were living before that. So that's all we know, they gave us their names and their morals and beliefs. Their values, their way to live, what's good or bad, their laws. That's all we know, so we think it's normal and it can't be changed. We don't know what was normal before we became slaves. All we were taught was how our ancestors lived as slaves and after, not before. So, we don't even know what to go back to. We living under their rules, laws, and beliefs, they gave to us. People that never loved us and taught us not to love each other. They took away our faith, hope, and love. They taught us greed, jealousy, and power. They took GOD out and took everything HE made and corrupted it. To make money and personal gain. But without love it means nothing. We need love, but a lot of us don't even love our self. So, we can't love no one else. We live by what we see on tv and movies and compare how we look and live by what we see.

It's getting darker and darker every day, so I call out to GOD and I pray. Let YOUR light shine Bright through me and show me what to do and what to say. I didn't hear no voice but I knew the answer was already written in HIS word. Just read, understand, put it in your heart, and learn to obey. HIS word not man's words, because HIS is the truth. HE has seen the misery of our people, HE has heard all our crying out because of the way we've been being treated. HE is concerned about how we're being treated. So, tell them and don't be afraid. I will be with you. The people that supposed to, will listen to continue, and what we killed each other for want nothing.

We need to humble ourselves and put our pride to the side. Quit thinking about just ourselves and think about coming together, and be able to agree on our purpose GOD's plan and the next generations that's coming behind us. We can stop this crazy way we thinking so it can change. It's been a long time coming but things gone change, we gone realize it's not about fortune and fame. It's about our GOD and to honor HIS plan so we can unite together and let our plans become the same. We have to be strong in our Lord and in the power of HIS might. Stand, gird your waist with the truth, put on the breast plate of righteousness, have your feet planted in gospel of peace, above all, take the shield of faith, so we can block all those wicked, evil thoughts their planting in our minds, and take the helmet of salvation, and the sword of the spirit, which is the word of our GOD, pray and watch over one another. We need GOD and we need each other. When I hear a lot of people saying I don't need nobody, I don't need no help "That's selfish, pride". We have to humble ourselves, quit thinking about just ourselves. That's how the enemy want us to think. Got us competing against each other. To get some fake fame and their fake money and material things. Which doesn't last forever. We have to realize we're fighting and killing each other to gain or win something that's fake, that's not going to last forever. We just doing what was planted in our minds by some wicked, evil people over 400 years ago, I know I kept repeating that but it's important. We don't care who we hurt as long as we gain or win whatever we want. Don't care about what the other person is going through, about their family, about nothing but what you want. Not what GOD want, and not how it's hurting people that loved or depended on them. Don't think or just don't care about the consequences.

How can the police kill somebody and say they was afraid or they thought the person was reaching for a gun. Not get charged but we can't? Why we can't shoot nobody when we scared for our life, like they can. We get scared just like them. The law's different for them, they above the law. It's people doing 20 to life for doing the same thing the police did or something less. Some of them were scared for their life when they did what they did. The only difference was they wasn't a police officer. When you become police, you get the right to kill someone and not go to jail. If you're afraid for your life but if you're not police you can't. What's the difference the people in jail only had seconds to make their decision too. It been videos of police beating or killing people and the videos showed the police was not in danger. If they were in danger. They supposed to be good marksman, they should be able to shoot someone in the leg or the arm. Not empty their clip, it should only take one shot. They shouldn't aim for chest or head; they definitely shouldn't shoot them in their back or when they're on the ground. How could they be scared for their life then. But they still get off, even if it's recorded. All they have to say is they was afraid for their life, I thought they were reaching for something, or they were resisting arrest. They still don't have to kill them, they have tasers, batons, rubber bullets, all types of defenses. But the first thing they think about is killing the person. They not trying to just stop the person and arrest them, after the person is down they keep beating them or shooting them until they run out of bullets. If you shoot someone once or twice, how could you still be scared? The police say if one of us shoot someone multiple times it was personal. Especially if they have been trained to do their job, they're trained to shoot at a target range. They know how to shoot their target why not shoot them in leg or arm. All the videos I saw it just looked like they were trying to kill that person. Not one looked like they were trying to arrest nobody, they wasn't trying to secure the situation, it looked like they wanted to just kill that person. Especially if they shooting until their gun empty, shooting deadly shots aiming for the head.

They're not shoots just to slow the person down. It's police that done killed more than one person and they are still police. To me they just like a gang when they kill somebody their reputation get bigger. How can they be scared at something they been thorough it before, they might tried it and liked it. Like a serial killer, but it's easier when they know they can get away with it. How do the people that hire the police know how their going to react under pressure or are they racist or just got a lot of anger built up in them and want to hurt and kill people? How do they know or do they even care? Because once they become a police, you part of their gang and they don't want their gang to look bad, so they down for each other. Even if they right or wrong, they going to figure out away to make it seem right. Even if it's a million of us that saw the same video they saw, and all million of us say the police was in the wrong. They just tell us they wasn't and that's it, they don't even have to explain why. They don't even tell us what they saw in the video, they don't even explain what happen in the video. Like they don't care what we think, like we don't have to explain why to us, this is what we decided just accept it. What you gone do protest, good we'll be able to tear gas you, shoot you with rubber bullets, take you to jail, give you citations, and still kill someone else when we want to.

So just accept it you can't do nothing about it. All the police have to say is they were scared for their life, but not why they was even putting their self in that situation if they were scared anyway. Most of the time the crime that they think the person did ain't even that serious of a crime that deserves being killed for. They be misdemeanors not even felonies, they kill people that, deserve if their guilty, a ticket. Most of the time the police not trying to arrest them because they robbed, kidnapped, or murdered someone. The stuff this people are being killed for things that don't even be serious crimes. The police have the right to kill someone just because the person didn't do what the police told them to do. Just because the officer felt like they got disrespected. They can kill someone because they think the person has a gun. If they are wrong and the person didn't have a gun, it's ok, it was just a mistake. They treat it like spilled coffee, when somebody is dead, that had a family, people that loved them. Yet they treat it like it wasn't nothing but a mistake. The officer just thought something that it wasn't. The court say the officer is still telling the truth. How many people have been beat or killed by the police? Way more than the ones caught on video, and none have been sentenced to go to jail, that I heard about. How many times have we had to march, protest, and riot? And nothing has changed.

The police still beating and killing, and not going to jail. We should see that's not working, we must come up with a different solution. All we been doing is tearing up our own neighborhood. I don't see how it's hurting the people we trying to hurt, they neighborhood still nice. I think the bus boycott got their attention more than the riot. They can arrest people that riot but can't arrest or make you get on their bus. Myself think we should stop spending money with them and stop working for them and stop entertaining them. I don't think it's going to be easy, like over night, but with GOD it can be done. Put GOD in the center and plan around HIM. Because we've been depending on them every since they brought us over here as their slaves. We don't know how to make it on our own and they know that, they let us make money but we spend it with them for everything we need. But we did live without them before they brought us over here and they taught us we need them to live. Like animals in the zoo, were taught to depend and listen to the zoo keeper. But the same kind of animals living in the wilderness and jungles living on their own. They learned how to survive, GOD put it in them when HE created them, just like HE did us. The things we depend on them for, we can do for ourselves. We can grow our own food, go fishing, raise our on meat, and build our own community. We, our ancestors, the ones that put the most work in building what they got now. We can do the same for ourselves while we depending on them. We talking about defunding the police when it's our taxes that's paying them, they taking our money and we have no say in what's it used for,. That's probably why they killing people they think don't have a job paying taxes. I think we all should quit buying their things and quit working for them, then how the police gone get paid. It sounds impossible but with GOD anything is possible. GOD created everything we need to survive before HE created us. These greedy people just stole, killed, and used people to get what they got. It wasn't even the ones that own it now. It was their ancestors that just passed it down to them. All they doing is taking advantage of what their ancestors left them. All they doing is trying to keep what they was taught going, no matter what it takes. That's all they know, and that's all they taught us. They don't see nothing wrong with it because it's all they know. They never had to live or been in the situation we're in. They can't understand something they never had to experience. You can just imagine them and the people they grew up around. Never worried about what they were gone eat, where they gone live, or how they were going to pay for nothing. That's why they don't understand why we live the way we do or do the things we do. But they make rules for us, they tell us right and wrong. When they don't know nothing about what we going thorough. Only what their ancestors taught them or what the media say. All the police have to do is say they were scared for their life and that's good for them, because they think were all crimanels and their lives are more important than ours. They have the power to say or wrong, we don't, we have some innocent people in jail and they have some guilty police that's not in jail. They just have us believing their more superior than us, we have no confidence when we face them. All they have is unity and we don't, they come together in time of need. While we against each other, either telling or even killing each other. You don't hear to much about a police killing another police. Because they from a different area or they wearing a different color. They one big gang down for each other, while we have many gangs that don't care about the other.

www.ingramcontent.com/pod-product-compliance
Lightning Source LLC
LaVergne TN
LVHW041715060526
838201LV00043B/747